Principles of Authentic Business:

Create a Sustainable Livelihood from the Heart

2nd Edition

By George Kao

Authentic Business Coach

www.GeorgeKao.com

This is an unusual Copyright Information page...

I, George Kao, give you permission to copy/paste any part of this book and share it anywhere online or offline, as long as you adhere to the license below.

CC0 1.0 Universal (CC0 1.0) -- Public Domain Dedication

No Copyright
The person who associated a work with this deed has dedicated the work to the public domain by waiving all of his or her rights to the work worldwide under copyright law, including all related and neighboring rights, to the extent allowed by law. You can copy, modify, distribute and perform the work, even for commercial purposes, all without asking permission. In no way are the patent or trademark rights of any person affected by CC0, nor are the rights that other persons may have in the work or in how the work is used, such as publicity or privacy rights.

Unless expressly stated otherwise, the person who associated a work with this deed makes no warranties about the work, and disclaims liability for all uses of the work, to the fullest extent permitted by applicable law.

When using or citing the work, you should not imply endorsement by the author or the affirmer.

Read more about the license here:
https://creativecommons.org/publicdomain/zero/1.0/
It's important to me that these ideas get out into the world and implemented, so that more people can succeed with their own authentic business.

--George Kao

How to Use This Book

I hope that this book of short essays will inspire you on your journey of creating and growing your authentic business.

You don't have to start at the beginning. Skip around the book as you wish!

Glance at the table of contents: which chapter jumps out to you at the moment? Flip there and enjoy.

At the end of each chapter there's a link to a companion video that will add nuance to the chapter. I encourage you to watch the video and add a comment below it, if you'd like.

I truly hope this book makes a positive difference in your business!

As you apply the ideas from the book and experience improvements in your authentic business, I'd love to hear about it – contact me via my website.

George Kao

www.GeorgeKao.com

A Note for Paperback Readers

Throughout, there are words and phrases that will be clickable in the digital copy of the book.

You can purchase the digital copy via Amazon for a lower price than the paperback.

If you don't mind reading a web-based version, you can view the whole digital book, complete with links, here – www.smpl.ro/principlesbook – all lower case.

Please keep the link private, as it's only for those who have bought the book.

Thank you, and enjoy!

–George Kao

***

Table of Contents

Authentic Business Success: Prioritize Your Inner Life

"Tell me about your goals."

"Well, I want a business beyond my wildest dreams. Doesn't everyone?!"

In her voice, there's a slight tinge of desperation… an unspoken, *"I refuse to be happy until I arrive."*

I had that same type of energy when I started my business in 2009. Easily influenced by my business mentors, I became uber-focused on external success. Becoming a millionaire, building a guru online presence, etc.

Eventually, I burned out. I came to realize that prioritizing the external often erodes the internal, and leads to constant comparison, grasping, lack of fulfillment, physical stress, etc. A breathless chasing after external validation.

Today, I wish to be *average* in external metrics, yet *lead* from the inner qualities.

In an industry of business coaches and marketing experts who all clamor for seven-figure incomes and million-follower fame, I focus on three other metrics of success now…

1. To become ever more skillful at my craft.

I work consistently to grow my abilities *to teach and coach*, as well as improve my subject-matter expertise of building an authentic business, which include:

- Authentic Content Marketing

- Joyful Productivity

- Clarifying Framework & Core Message

- Product-Market Fit (what I call Better Offers)

- Paid Advertising (e.g. Facebook Ads, LinkedIn Ads)

- Netcaring (a heart-based way of networking)

- Online Course Creation & Marketing

- Simple Book Creation & Self-Publishing

The more skillful I become in these areas, the more my clients and students benefit.

The more *they* benefit, the more fulfilled I feel.

Word-of-mouth spreads, resulting in even more inspiration to improve my craft.

It is a virtuous cycle that helps everyone.

Compare this to my previous set of priorities:

Focusing on money and audience growth creates a vicious cycle of always wanting more in the **external** metrics, and always chasing, yet never quite accessing a consistent fulfillment in one's work.

Fixation on external ambitions tends to cause desperation, manipulation, disappointment, and worst of all, a disconnection from one's internal source of joy.

Flaunting our success (the usual way influencers market themselves) can also evoke envy in others, and hubris within ourselves.

The fact is, the **more** material things you have (or the more attention you get), the **less** there is for others. This is not a "limiting belief" but a *physical law* – the conservation of energy.

Therefore, I try to have *enough* money, *enough* attention, rather than always "more".

On the other hand, there is something else that is truly limitless: internal ambitions and "success" in the inner qualities. This inspires others, and brings benefit to all who are touched by your life.

2. To grow in the inner qualities.

It's not just about making money or even making an impact. I see work *itself* as a stage for personal development.

Every moment, whether I am writing a chapter like this, or taking care of administrative duties, or talking with a client, all of it is an opportunity to practice virtues such as:

- Awareness

- Blessing

- Compassion

- (I've written a series about my "spiritual alphabet" on the Soul Gym FB Page)

As often as I can, I "breathe" one of these virtues into my activities each day.

If I ever find myself thinking, "I just have to get this done," I realize I have lost touch with the higher purpose of that activity.

It's never just about "getting something done", even if I am doing something as mundane as cleaning the toilet. It is an opportunity given to me by life to practice mindfulness, being mindful of the inner qualities that can be developed (or eroded) in that very moment.

By focusing on the higher purpose of work, I find a deeper fulfillment in anything I do.

3. To improve my balance.

As my business evolves, so does my schedule.

It is always a work in progress, finding a good balance in work, rest, and hobbies.

In work, I seek higher purpose.

In rest, I renew myself for further work.

In hobbies, I stretch my creativity in new directions.

These three core areas are important to many of us. (If you have family to take care of, various duties can fit into the above categories, sometimes work, sometimes rest, sometimes hobbies, and some can be done together as a family.)

Without working on your balance, these can happen:

- Burnout (too much work)

- Financial stress (not enough value-creating-work)

- Lack of fulfillment (not enough hobbies or purpose-awareness in work)

Life is always giving us new challenges to balance these spheres.

***

To recap, the top three priorities in my business are:

- To become more skillful at my craft.

- To grow in the inner qualities.

5

- To improve my balance between work, rest, and hobbies.

They are often unmeasurable, not the kind of KPI's (key performance indicators) that most entrepreneurs measure.

In the external (and enviable) ways—income and attention—I wish to be average. However, as a business coach, I work to pull up everyone else around me in these outer metrics, helping them attain a sustainable income. However, I also wish to inspire them with a desire to grow in the inner qualities as well.

May you match your own priorities with what truly, deeply fulfills you.

Watch the companion video for this chapter here:

www.bit.ly/abp2ch12

Light Marketing

I'm going to introduce a phrase that I'll begin using occasionally – "light marketing" or "lightside marketing" – to represent the kind of marketing I aim to practice.

What might come to mind by the word "light" is that it's ineffective. That's not what I mean by it, of course. In fact, Light Marketing is more likely to be sustainable for a solopreneur. The consistency of showing up – lightly! – then brings greater effectiveness over time, and a grounded Self-confidence, compared to doing heavy marketing which tends to burn us out and make us avoid doing marketing altogether.

Here are the two facets of Light Marketing…

Light Effort

The key to Light Marketing is light effort with each marketing activity.

Whether we are creating and posting content, or announcing our services to our social media audience, we do it all with lightness of touch. In my joyful productivity course I call this "working lightly".

Why is that more effective, you might say, compared to "getting it right the first time and making a splash"?

Because marketing is a skill that's developed with a lot of practice, and most solopreneurs have the fantasy that they can just get it right from the get go, when in reality, they are more likely to make a splat than a splash…

So once again, bring lightness to each marketing activity. Yes, bring minimal effort. Work lightly. Don't take any one post, offer, campaign so seriously! See it all as an ongoing process of exploration and experimentation.

It's not that we're trying to be sloppy or overly casual. By doing Light Marketing we simply understand that excellence is a long-term, continuous practice of kaizen.

Also, and this is key – by reducing the effort in one's self-promotions, we save time and and energy which can then go into improving our products and services. I've come to increasingly see the wisdom of this – avoid any solopreneur who tries too hard to market... that time was spent away from improving their service.

The Light Side of the Force

Light Marketing is also meant to be contrasted with the "the dark side" of marketing…

Unfortunately, dark marketing is how most marketing is done and taught – based on persuasion psychology, neuromarketing – and basically, cleverly manipulating people until they buy from you.

Disingenuous sales funnels, pressure-filled scarcity tactics, and bait-and-switch content.

Even though those cynical strategies "work" to "convert" people into buyers sometimes, it tends not to build a long-term loyal audience.

For sure, it brings more deception and anxiety (fear of missing out) into the world. It doesn't make the world more beautiful, even if it temporarily makes money.

Light Marketing, on the other hand, takes more patience in the beginning, but then over time, it gets easier and easier to make money because you'll have an increasingly loyal audience who is willing to share about your content and offerings. Their trust in you will be well-deserved.

Hold Lightly

I practice holding lightly to ideas. This means I'll allow this concept of Light Marketing to continue evolving, seeing how it may become truly useful to others.

I also very much welcome anyone to use this phrase. If you find Light Marketing truly useful, please do use it anywhere.

En-joy 

Watch the companion video and add any comments here:

www.bit.ly/abp2ch15

The Three Paths of Solopreneurship: Wait to Respond – Funnel Hustle – and The Middle Way of Authentic Business

In my 13 years of coaching solopreneurs, I've noticed 3 ways that people approach solopreneurship:

Wait to Respond

The way that most service providers build their businesses is to just wait for random word-of-mouth. You might get a few clients a year, if you're lucky. Some might be a great fit, and some will not be. Maybe you recognize yourself here. There is no judgment, just clarity which can help you make choices more consciously.

Why do people take this approach? Because starting a business is, understandably, so overwhelming as well as confronting (to one's self-esteem) that sometimes, we cannot bring ourselves to do any marketing.

Yet, with this path, it can take 10 or 15 years (maybe longer) to gain enough client experience to become confident in your work. Or to finally get so tired of waiting for clients to come to you that you decide to swing to the other side of the spectrum and try to follow a rigorous business strategy.

You might then get sold into the typical marketing approach, which is…

Funnel Hustling

A "funnel" in the marketing sense can be seen as a plan to guide unsuspecting consumers through a carefully-crafted process in order to convince them to make a purchase.

The term "hustle" has various definitions – to work yourself to the bone, to persuade or convince someone, or to acquire money by unscrupulous means.

Therefore, what I'm calling "funnel hustling" (the mainstream way of approaching solopreneurship), is to work overly hard to create a manipulative set of steps – a "funnel" – that's supposed to get you clients and make money easily.

What's specifically involved in funnel hustling? Clarifying audience personas so that you can speak to the emotional drivers that make them want to buy. You do this through persuasive copywriting and visual branding that makes the potential client salivate. You'll probably spend lots of money trying to do all of that, to try to charm and enroll people. Maybe you'll even make promises in your marketing that you aren't confident about keeping. This is how mainstream funnel hustling is taught.

With this path to solopreneurship, if you're lucky, you'll make money – but it's not guaranteed and can feel tenuous – and even if you make a lot of money, the profit isn't there because you've spent so much on consultants and freelancers and software. In other words, you've spent a lot of money to make a lot of money and there's not much left at the end of the hard work.

The Funnel Hustling path exhibits these traits:

- Artificial

- Trying to be instantly impressive

- A fixed mindset

- Very costly

- Huge risk

Following this path, it's easy to fall for advertisements that promise that if certain funnels are set up, the system will work for you like an ATM machine: you'll be able to earn as much money as you want. You just need to spend more on the marketing.

What I've seen from the solopreneurs on this path is, sadly, costly failures.

Mainstream marketing is basically this path. Most solopreneurs with slick-looking websites and polished social media brands feel like they're putting up a wall to hide behind – to hide their authentic expression.

The Middle Way

The third (and middle) way of solopreneurship is to actively and intentionally walk the path of growth mindset in your marketing.

With the understanding that your potential is unlimited, you:

- Practice intentionally

- Show up consistently

On this middle path to solopreneurship, you get more skillful in your creativity and service over time.

To be sustainable on this path requires your dedication to joyful productivity – being consistent in your efforts to work and infuse that work with your deeper values while maintaining a gentle attitude towards the outcomes of your work.

With the middle path, your growth is more manageable. You can keep the promises you make in your marketing. You can be more intentional about whom you take on, and you'll have more inquiries than the path of just waiting.

Some might call this the path of "marketing enlightenment". It's a state of not caring about things that we ought not to give a [__] about, such as what people think of us, or trying to project a puffed up version of ourselves.

This is the path that I teach. It's the path of authentic business. Together, we aim to focus on personal growth within the actions we take for our businesses. As a result, we feel more organic and sustainable than if we pursue (or have pursued) the Funnel Hustling path.

Again, the core components of the Middle Way is about consistently showing up, practicing your authentic expression, and practicing your heartfelt service to humanity. This builds trust over time with your audience. And with yourself.

On this path, we're always investigating two questions:

- What content am I putting out there that my ideal audience finds most interesting?

- What offers am I putting out there that clients find most exciting and helpful?

With ongoing practice of increasing your skillfulness in these areas, you gradually become so good that your ideal audience can no longer ignore you. No matter how many times in the past they've scrolled past your content or offers, eventually, your presence becomes so resonant for them, and the word of mouth so strong, that they will have to take a serious look.

By taking this path day-to-day, step-by-step, you are becoming stronger and more resilient. You are becoming more of a master of authentic business.

Watch the companion video and add any comments
here:

www.bit.ly/abp2ch3

I used to dream of Financial Freedom…

I used to dream of "financial freedom"… having so much money that I could just do whatever I wanted, travel the world, give money abundantly to causes and people in need.

I invested in lots of business programs that sold me on that dream.

Eventually I realized two things…

(1) The ones selling the dreams were the ones getting rich… not those of us buying into the programs. (Unless we also joined their ranks, and sold dreams of easy and big money to others.)

(2) By getting caught up in that culture of hype, I was actually delaying the building of my right livelihood.

Thankfully I woke up to these dynamics and stopped buying into those programs for a decade now. Since then, I've worked diligently to build what I feel today is my truest livelihood yet.

When I am well-rested, feeling loved, and connected to my higher self, I realize that what I *really* want isn't financial freedom…

What I yearn for is the feeling of being truly useful to others, experiencing my strengths in service of uplifting humanity, and feeling that the money I earn is honest and noble.

Yet when I feel tired, or fearful, or discouraged, then the hype of financial freedom can tempt me again.

Perhaps the most important and urgent thing in the pursuit of our authentic businesses and lives therefore, is to reconnect to our higher selves. We all need self-care and spiritual practices that bring us back to a deeper perspective of what Life is really about.

When we're reconnected in that way, we might see that there is much opportunity (and urgency) for us to earn a *truly worthwhile* living, to be of service as we make money, doing work that co-creates a world that our hearts long for.

Mahatma Gandhi named the seven destructive forces in society:

- Wealth Without Work

- Pleasure Without Conscience

- Knowledge Without Character

- Commerce Without Morality

- Science Without Humanity

- Religion Without Sacrifice

- Politics Without Principle

Notice from this list that there's only one sector of society Gandhi mentions twice: how money is acquired.

Is the primary goal of work to satisfy our own desires? If so, then it can become easy to get obsessed about passive income and financial freedom.

What if, instead, we find the purpose of work to be calling us to a deeper life?

I believe that to hear that call, we need to be rested, renewed, and connected to our higher selves…

We can then uplift our perspective, and see that perhaps the primary purpose of work is something deeper, such as contribution and character. That what we do for others also builds our virtues, and that one of the results of work is to build our financial security.

I am grateful that today, I have finally built a business that I love, allowing me to feel that I'm of genuine service to others, while growing personally and professionally.

This is what I yearn for you:

To deeply LOVE your work, your business, so much that you aren't fixated on financial freedom or passive income. To feel so deeply that you are earning a right livelihood, that offers of wealth no longer hold the allure they once did.

Here's an interesting thought: When you are vacationing or taking a break from your business with your passive income, others are finding ways to add better value to your ideal audience. When you're *not* improving your products or services, other people *are* improving theirs.

Let's look at market competition not from a fearful state, but rather see it as an inspiration for our continual personal and professional development. We are called to become better and better, to innovate and improve our products/services, to become increasingly valuable to our ideal audience.

The fixation on financial freedom erodes the commitment to our true livelihood.

This illusion that is being sold to you, of a stable offering that always makes you money and never changes—is that true of life?

In the conventional worldview, work is only a **means** to the real purpose of having more vacations and fulfilling our desires. This eventually puts you on the hedonic treadmill of materialism.

Or, a more altruistic version of this conventional worldview is that you should make lots of money so that you can have the power to choose the good causes that get funded. Still, it's about control and ego.

Here is an alternative idea:

Vacations, breaks, and self-care are a way to renew ourselves, to reconnect to our higher selves, so that we can come back to work and improve our offerings, making them even better for our audience. Vacations allow us the renewed energy and perspective to work wisely, to earn money in ways that feel ever more noble to us.

"Work" and "making money" don't have to be necessary evils. Our money-earning actions can be transformed into our heartfelt cause for the betterment of the world and our own personal development.

Instead of obsessing about financial freedom, let us see other people's payments to us as a doorway to sacred reciprocity: for us to do our best work for them.

The phrase "having it all: usually means "Having lots of money and plenty of free time." This concept is an illusion promoted by those who get rich selling you that dream.

I offer an alternative definition of what it means to "have it all" —

"Earning money by expressing your strengths to uplift others, practicing your joyful productivity, continually growing in meaningful ways, and having a rhythm of self-care that keeps you refreshed and connected to your highest self."

Not as concise… but perhaps more balanced, true and even better…within reach

I wish for you everything that brings you true alignment with the highest version of yourself, and with your deepest sense of purpose.

Watch the companion video and add any comments here:

www.bit.ly/abp2ch11

To get attention authentically, practice demonstrating your care…

In marketing it is assumed that the goal, the daily effort, is to *get more views, more followers, more sales….* always wanting other people to *do more* of what **we** want them to do.

Conventional marketing is very self-centered.

"If I don't strive to get my share of attention, I won't be able to survive!"

The result is the proliferation of questionable marketing strategies and pushy sales tactics, that aim to "grab" audience attention and persuade them to action.

The real problem? It seems to work in the short term. The squeaky wheel at first gets the grease. But eventually, all that squeaking gets annoying and it gets replaced!

Short-term strategies will come back to haunt the marketers who use them.

It's this selfish core of *"I want you to do this"* that makes consumers distrust and dislike so much of marketing. Whether it's the emails that clutter our inbox, or the pushy calls to action, we feel we "have" to consume marketing, in order to get to the good stuff—the content we signed up for.

The bottom line: Most marketers *don't care enough*—they're just blasting their promotions to everyone, hoping to catch a few. They don't care enough to slow down and target their communications thoughtfully. It feels interruptive, a necessary evil—which is why adblocker browser plugins are so popular.

Instead of "how can we get more attention", let's think in terms of *"how can we show that we care?"*

There is a deep calling within us – authentic business owners – to bring more love and wisdom into the business world.

By bringing true caring to our audience, the natural reciprocity is loyal attention, deeply happy customers, and greater word of mouth.

Caring more for our current readers, subscribers, and the clients we already have, means that we will want to grow a deeper understanding of *who they are* and *what they're going through* right now. We can then create content and offerings that are more relevant to them.

This way, everybody wins.

Care enough to seek conversation.

What are they thinking about now? How do they feel about our industry and the offerings that are available in the market? What can we do to meet them where they are… so we can serve them better?

Willingness to care means willingness to talk to them. To converse 1–1 with as many of them as possible.

Reach out privately to those who engage with our content on social media. Individually contact some of our email subscribers to get to know them better. Not just sending out surveys, but caring enough to be in 1–1 conversation with them.

In our conversations, try to uncover what it is they are struggling with now: what can we create that will help them? Find out what related products/services they've bought. What did they love, and what weren't they satisfied with? This helps us create – or curate! – better offerings for them.

Most of us business owners are so in our own heads (and hearts), absorbed with our own experiences, in love with our own modality, focused on promoting our own ideas, that we can easily lose touch with what the audience **actually** wants.

Care enough to risk rejection.

Reaching out to people doesn't mean they'll get back to you. Or if they do, they might not be interested in talking with you.

Still, the fact that they're in your audience (email subscribers, followers and friends on social media) – means that they resonated with your energy signature enough to stay. Reach out with care, whether or not they respond right away.

We need to care more about our audience than our concern for possible embarrassment by their silence or rejection.

Keep returning to these questions:

- How can I show my audience that I care?

- How can I better understand them?

This is how real trust and loyal attention are created. Not by trying to *grab* attention. By demonstrating caring, others naturally trust and become loyal to you.

Care enough to keep a healthy schedule

May we also care so deeply about our mission, our opportunity to serve our audience with our content and offerings, that we are careful to maintain a healthy schedule.

Without a focused effort towards a stable schedule as a solopreneur, we are prone to get drawn into rabbit holes of research, content consumption, or even, ironically, "caring" for others.

Wait, didn't I just say we should care more? Yes, but to care in a way that allows us to have the greatest, deepest, positive impact with our mission.

This means that sometimes, we do have to say "no" when others ask us for favors or to help them with this or that random thing. We say "no" because we care about keeping good boundaries. We care enough to be very mindful of how we use our heart and energy for the more effective ways to care for our audience and clients.

The Authentic Way to Become an Influencer

Most influencers compete for attention by trying to be *more entertaining*, *more shocking*, *more clever* with their content.

Instead, we can instead aim to be our authentic caring selves—rather than trying to be polished.

We can win by caring more for our audience than other influencers are willing to care.

We do this by deeply understanding our audience, which then allows us to create content and offerings that **they will also care about.**

I dream of a world where influencers and thought leaders will prioritize their own inner growth over their external metrics.

Don't try to "grab attention" and "get" millions of followers. Focus on caring enough for your true fans, by seeking deeper conversation with them, and your business will naturally thrive.

Watch the companion video and add any comments
here:

www.bit.ly/abp2ch14

10 Year Plan for Authentic Business

Here is a plan to help you create a business that expresses your soul -- and allows you to have a semi-retirement lifestyle.

What's possible with this plan:

- Year 2: Part-time income with providing your authentic service.

- Year 4: Full-time income by providing both 1-1 and group offerings.

- Year 10: Full-time income, somewhat passively, allowing for semi-retirement, and being one of the best in your field.

Although this is called a 10-Year Plan, you might be able to speed things up. It depends on your time management and consistency of action. This is why I consider joyful productivity to be the foundation for authentic business growth.

10 years allows a spacious and realistic way for most solopreneurs to realize this dream, by developing good habits, bit by bit.

If you currently have a full-time job, or if you have responsibilities for caretaking, the first 2 years of the plan may take you longer, as you get used to creating healthy boundaries in your business and life.

Without further ado, here is the plan…

Year 1: Authentic Content Marketing

To begin, focus your efforts on building an audience of kindred spirits, people who resonate with your authentic voice and style:

- Using a blog and/or video channel, share your thoughts regarding your passions, learnings, and experiences. Explore your "voice" and ideas. Create a variety of content.

- Find a rhythm that works for you to do this consistently. Carve out a schedule of content-creation that doesn't interfere with your other responsibilities in work and life.

- Allow yourself to be authentic in your content, not trying to copy anyone, but doing it in a style that feels true to you. This is how your true fans will find you.

- Learn how to distribute your content -- otherwise nobody will be seeing it. The simplest way to distribute is through Facebook & Instagram Ads. (FYI I have a whole course on this stuff: Facebook Ads Course.)

- Occasionally, study the stats for your content: what's the average amount of engagement you're getting? Which pieces of content get above-average engagement? Try to create more content like that, and yet, keep experimenting with the expression of your authentic voice.

- For a comprehensive content plan, study this course: Authentic Content Flow.

In the first two years, I also recommend working eagerly on your joyful productivity habits. This is foundational. It allows you to work with efficiency, calm focus, and a healthy balance of work, rest, and play.

Year 2: One-to-One Services

While continuing your rhythm of authentic content marketing, now also make yourself available to your audience for 1–1 services, such as coaching, counseling, consulting, healing, mentoring, or being a freelancer.

Providing services is the **quickest** way to start creating a meaningful income. And, it's the best way for you to learn what really works, and what types of people you love to help through your services.

Consider the tapering strategy for getting your first clients.

If you are in no rush to build an income, and prefer to sell something more passive, that takes less of your time, then skip down to the actions in Year 3 which involve creating a group program, or Year 4, building an online course. Then you can come back to offering 1-1 services when you have more time to spend in your business.

Tips for 1-1 services:

- Make it easier for your clients to schedule or reschedule with you by using software such as Google Calendar Scheduling or Calendly. This also allows you to automate reminder emails (or text messages) to them.

- Begin to create client case studies. Take on the mindset of creating real transformation for clients. This will speed up your learning and get you more referrals.

Year 3: Group Program (maybe also a Book)

By this point, you'll have created at least a part-time income. You might now be able to quit your job, or switch to a part-time position. If you're a caretaker, you can now hire some help for your children, parents, or others you're caring for. This allows you to spend more time on your business.

In this year, while you continue your content rhythm, and your 1-1 client work, you'll also now create a group offering.

Combining your 1-1 services with a Group Program helps you to achieve a full-time income. For example, perhaps you now have 10 one-to-one clients paying

$300 per month, equalling $3,000 per month income for you. Now, you are also enrolling 20 members into a group program where they each pay $150 per month, which combined with your 1-1 income creates a total of $6,000 per month of income for your business.

A group program is a wonderful alternative to offer people who aren't ready for your 1-1 work. You can also offer it to your 1-1 clients who are completing their package, and are ready to move into a maintenance-mode in their work with you.

However, enrolling enough clients into a group is only possible after you've gotten traction with your marketing, which is why I recommend this for Year 3.

You might offer a group coaching program where you facilitate a call every week, along with an ongoing private Facebook group to facilitate mutual support among members, and for you to answer questions.

To see an example of how I structure this, check out the description page for my MasterHeart Business Program.

Once your group program is formed, you might want to *reduce* your 1–1 client load, so that you have more time for the group program.

At this point, you've created a lot of content, so you might also want to put together your first book… it doesn't have to be complicated! You can simply collect your existing writings into one long document. Then, organize it so there's some kind of flow, and then fill in any missing gaps. This is how I've been able to write 4 books!

I simply organized my best posts—that I've already written—into themes, and then organize them into books, and self-publish using Amazon's KDP service.

If you'd like a comprehensive plan for creating and marketing your books, take my online course: Simple Self-Publishing.

Now that you've been engaging with your fans for a few years, notice who shares your content, and who signs up for your services and programs. You are starting to understand who your true fans are.

Going forward, focus on making your content and offerings for your true fans -- write and speak with them in your mind and heart -- and more of them will find you!

Year 4: Online Courses

During this year, get up and running with your own online courses, which will be the foundation of your semi-retirement.

A few tips:

For years, you've learned deeply and widely in your field—by creating content, doing 1–1 services, and offering group programs. You have case studies that demonstrate that your modality, or process, and framework indeed works for your ideal clients.

This is why I put Online Courses into Year 4. Having the abundant experience of serving clients and seeing what works (and doesn't work) allows your online courses to be more impactful and credible. If however you find it easier to teach instead of providing 1-1 services, perhaps due to your schedule, then it's ok to move your course creation up to Year 2.

What I'm referring to here is creating low-priced ($30 - $300) do-it-yourself online courses so that people can benefit from your experience and personality, without you having to be there.

One of the common blocks I hear: "I feel that I need to be there for the students in order for them to really benefit."

If you're struggling with that, consider these questions:

- When you read books, do you ever blame the author for "not being there with you" to answer your questions immediately?

- When you watch videos online, do you expect instant interaction with the creator?

A low-priced, DIY online course is similar to these: It's a video and/or audio series that includes some written content. Students should be able to submit questions to you, but you don't have to be there immediately. It's perfectly acceptable to take a few days to respond to them. They'll be grateful for your personal response.

As we'll see later, you can eventually delegate these responses as well, as you grow a team, so that you can semi-retire.

To go deep and learn my methods, check out my online course for how to create/market your own courses.

You'll now have several streams of income:

- 1–1 services

- Group programs

- Online courses

- Possibly books as well

As you read this chapter, are you coming across any internal blocks or concerns that this "couldn't work" for you? Let me know by adding a comment – I'll remind you where to do that at the end of the chapter. I'd be happy to hear from you.

Year 5: Scaling with Ads & Automation

Some might say that this is where your business "really" becomes a business, because your income has gotten to be much more stable and automated.

Now that you have online courses, you can use Facebook/Google Ads to reach tens of thousands of additional ideal audience members.

To learn my complete strategy for doing so, study my Facebook Ads Course.

You'll also benefit from starting to use software such as Zapier to automate recurring tasks in your business. I do this with many tasks so that I can stay a solopreneur instead of having a team, yet still be able to deliver more than 20 evergreen courses ongoingly.

Building an Authentic Business is not just "making more money" but making truly *good* money—from a deep sense of service to one's ideal audience, having the income emerge from a direct connection to one's meaningful work.

Year 6: Training Mentees

When you get to this point, you'll have hundreds (or thousands) of people taking your online courses. You'll start getting many requests for working with you 1–1 that you are unable to accommodate. Your group program might even be full at this point (as mine has been for more than a year.)

This is where it's important to have mentees to take over some (or all) of your 1–1 services, and/or to help you facilitate your group program so that it can expand. Here are the steps I suggest when you're at this stage:

- Make a list of your most ideal clients.

- Which of them are interested in doing the kind of work you've been doing?

- Start a mentoring program, with these individuals as your first mentees.

- You might even want to offer a certificate / certification by the end of it.

- Refer the people on your waiting list to your new mentees.

- True mentoring is where the mentee is doing the real work with real clients, yet have consultations with you to learn from challenging client situations, to keep improving their service.

Also, by this point, you may have a large enough audience such that you could create in-person gatherings (workshops / retreats / conferences / cruises) and be able to recruit enough people from your audience to make such events worthwhile. Many people try to do this too early on, and find it very difficult to fill their events.

Year 7: Hiring Your Assistants

By this point you have:

- A thriving group program

- Online courses with thousands of students

- Mentees to refer clients to

- You might still keep a few 1–1 clients if you'd like

- Perhaps some books you've published

With more than enough income at this point to meet your needs, it's time to focus on hiring and training assistants to take over the administrative tasks, so that you can free up more time to do your highest-level work.

Important -- Before you hire, I would recommend spending a year focusing on how you can automate more of your tasks. This is currently my focus. I do most of my automation with Zapier.

If you've already hired by this point, this year's focus is to create a more optimal working relationship with your assistant(s) so that it creates more time freedom for you. In fact, you might encourage your assistant to use automation software more skillfully, so that they can do the human tasks for you that bots don't do well.

One of the best places to recruit great assistants is your own audience of true fans. They know your work, and they love your style. There are undoubtedly some people in your audience who would love to work for you.

Year 8: Larger Joint Ventures

Now that you have a sizable audience from all your efforts at creating consistent content over the years, and scaling your courses with ads, you can now collaborate with the bigger players in your industry in so-called Joint Ventures (JVs) if you wish to.

Or, if you prefer not to do larger joint ventures, just skip forward to the following year's focus: Systems Documentation.

To scale your reach, consider creating telesummits (virtual conferences), co-created courses, and cross-promotions of courses or products.

Perhaps you'll also want to co-facilitate, and do joint marketing for in-person gatherings.

Such cross-pollination can grow the creativity of your business, and scale your reach to more ideal audiences compared to only using ads.

Your assistant can help you track these JVs and all the logistics involved.

When you get to this scale, and have any questions, reach out to me. I've done many JVs even before I started this 10-year plan. I've learned what kind of partners are best to seek, and how to do these partnerships simply and effectively.

You can get a shortcut to my learnings about JVs by taking my course: Authentic Joint Ventures and Simple Collabs.

Year 9: Systems Documentation

You're getting ready for semi-retirement.

This is the year to focus on making sure that just about everything done by your assistant(s) is documented in an organized and easy-to-consume way.

Your assistant(s) can create the training videos, written guides, and FAQ's, so that if they need to move onto other jobs, which will inevitably happen, your future team members can get up and running quickly, thanks to the step-by-step documentation that's now available.

Year 10: Kaizen Forever

Congratulations—you have reached the freedom of semi-retirement!

Why "semi" instead of "full" retirement?

Mahatma Gandhi said that the dream of "wealth without work" is one of the ills of society. I don't believe that full passive income has true integrity. There are still so many people struggling in the world that your business can help even more effectively, that it's your opportunity, and perhaps responsibility, to continually innovate and improve your services and products.

Plus, it's better for your physical and mental well-being to keep working, in the spirit of true service to your clients, customers, mentees, and your calling.

Kaizen is a Japanese word that means "continuous improvement".

I like to say Authentic Businesses are in "kaizen" forever because it can always be improved in its effectiveness of serving its customers, and its deepening of the fulfillment of your mission.

I encourage you to bookmark this chapter and set yourself a reminder to return every year and check-in on what to do next and reflect on your progress.

(Originally written in 2018. Updated in 2023.)

Watch the companion video and add any comments here:

www.bit.ly/abp2ch10

Venn Diagram for Authentic Business

In trying to understand your purposeful work, you may have encountered various complex venn diagrams to express the idea of Ikigai, the Japanese concept of a person's "reason for being."

Well, here's my version of one... a venn diagram for Authentic Business:

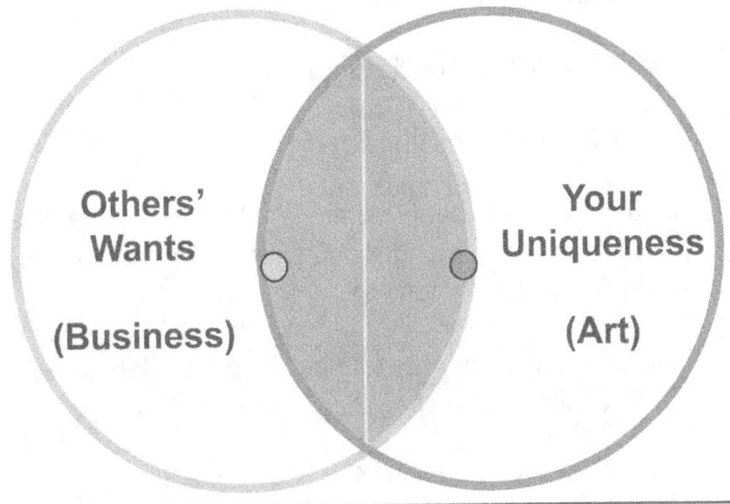

I created it in 2014, and I think it can still help many people to understand where to place their energies in their work.

The circle on the right represents your passions, which can be...

- Topics you love to talk about

- Problems you enjoy working on

- People you love to help (sometimes described as your "ideal client audience")

The circle on the left represents high-demand markets (what people are buying) and these tend to …

- Be hot, or popular, in the current culture

- Solve a painful problem

- Give instant gratification

- Be easy to consume

Most of us who are heart-based, idealistic people tend to start businesses in the right-hand circle. This means that the solutions we offer tend to:

- Take more time or require deeper work before results can be seen

- Be esoteric, or based in specialty knowledge, rather than popularly understood

- Be "deeper" or more spiritual

Here's the main issue for people like us – we expect results in the kind of timeline that usually only happens when we build our businesses with a focus on the left-hand circle.

Yet, we feel motivated only by the things in that right-side circle.

As a result, we find ourselves at extremes, leaning heavily towards the left circle in our hopes for results, but also leaning heavily towards the right circle in our energy and actions. To bring in some moderation – and some faster income – let's take a closer look at the diagram:

Notice the small green and gold dots.

The gold dot – which is at the edge of the green circle – represents business opportunities that are in higher demand, yet still within your circle of passion. It's not your biggest passion, but you can bring yourself to enjoy those activities.

The green dot (at the edge of the gold circle) stands for opportunities that are closer to your Passions but have less market demand.

If you currently have financial reserves or a stable income, you can start at the green dot, and with each new project, keep moving right – toward your truest Passions.

Does your business need to make money sooner? You'll have to start at the gold dot. This allows for quicker income while building your confidence. With each success, move gradually in the direction of the green dot.

Along the way, you'll also build an audience who will be more willing to move with you towards the center of your passion in the circle on the right.

Even if you pursue the gold dot first, delivering what's in demand, you can still flavor your work with your passion. For example, even though I teach online marketing, I am always bringing my passion for spiritual/personal development into my teaching. As a result, my brand carries more authenticity. That's what we're aiming for in our authentic businesses, right?

I hope this diagram will help you consider your current offerings, and how they relate to your passion versus what others want.

As you progress in your work experimentations, you will likely experience the increase of both success *and* fulfillment, represented by the purple part of the venn diagram.

Watch the companion video and add any comments here:

www.bit.ly/abp2ch2

The 12 Authentic Business Values

At the moment I'm writing this, I am launching my group program for solopreneurs who resonate with a certain set of values. By "solopreneur" I mean someone who is building a simple, low overhead business that supports them financially while allowing maximum freedom.

I'm happy to share these values statements with you. Perhaps it'll serve as an inspiration for your own journey as well.

As you read each point, take a moment to reflect on how it aligns with you. I'd love comments and questions – I share a link at the end of the chapter where you can add your reactions and thoughts.

1. My business is not just a way of making money. Instead, it feels like a **mission** or **cause**. The vision of the ripple effect my business could have is what inspires me to grow.

2. I'm dedicated to serving and uplifting humanity through ***the way*** I do business. I understand the necessity (and opportunity) for personal growth throughout the journey.

3. Marketing is not a means to an end. It's not only a way to get more clients. Authentic Marketing is an effective vehicle to evolve my understanding of my "calling" (fulfilling my career purpose), and to serve humanity through my **authentic content**.

4. I understand the importance of actively **distributing my content**, for example through collaborations or social media ads, as an essential way that my business makes a positive difference to my audience, industry, and world.

5. I'm dedicated to working with **joyful productivity**. It's part of my life's purpose to infuse my deeper values into my daily work. And to learn how to balance work with self-care, play, and other priorities in my life.

6. I believe in **healthy money** – relating to the world of finances in ways that support mental and societal health. While I aim to be responsible for my finances, I also practice letting go of fixation on the numbers. I prioritize the health of my relationships over the primacy of money. I aim to use money as a way to connect human beings for societal improvement.

7. I value **netcaring**, which is the ongoing practice of connecting *from the heart* with colleagues and clients, current and potential, with genuine enjoyment instead of agenda-laden networking. I love **collaboration**, or learning from colleagues (and clients) and exploring win-win relationships.

8. Instead of pushy sales, I **optimize my offerings** so that they are truly aligned and delightful for my audience. I continually conduct market research,

as I lean into my compassion for my audience, desiring to meet them where they're at.

9. I remind my audience of these aligned offers by consistently doing **gentle launches**. Therefore, my "promotions" feel more like friendly invitations (without attachment to their responses), instead of desperate attention-seeking.

10. Even when my business does well financially, I'm not complacent with the state of my products and services. I'm committed to the **mastery of my craft**, to continually upgrade the value I offer my customers and audience.

11. In our community we are tolerant and curious about **a diversity of perspectives**, political and religious (as well as apolitical and areligious), knowing that each person has barely a grain of understanding compared to the Truth which encompasses the whole. Therefore, we are **gentle, caring, and exploratory** in our communications with each other.

12. We practice bringing play into our work. We believe in the genius that can come from improvisation, experimentation, and humbly sharing our authentic Self with our audience. (Speaking of improvisation... this 12th value was created on the spot in this video.)

Which of these values do you resonate with most? I'm open to your feedback and ideas. Add a comment under this companion video:

www.bit.ly/abp2ch1

May all of us solopreneurs find more authentic and joyful success in our business!

Don't Niche Yourself.
DO Niche Your Offers.

A lot of us heart-based solopreneurs rebel against the advice that we have to find and commit to a niche, narrowing the vastness of our interests to solve a specific problem in the marketplace.

Perhaps we consider ourself to be a multipotentialite, integrating various modalities and fields into our work. Or we otherwise don't like to limit our identity.

I get it. I'm the same way. To say that I'm an "authentic business coach" is still very broad, and I teach classes in everything from authentic Ai to facebook ads to book publishing.

Notice that my offers are niched, but not my overall brand. This is the strategy I've been using for 14 years, so if you're niche-resistant, it's the advice I'll give to you as well.

For your personal brand, stay as broad as you'd like. You can simply describe your business based on values, and/or overall type of work (e.g. coaching, healing, etc), and/or your broader mission.

For each of your services, programs, products, events, get as specific as you are able to. A coach might create a webinar about overcoming blocks to career advancement in a specific industry, and a coaching package to help someone through the challenges they have with their family of origin. A healer might offer a service subscription for those dealing with chronic fatigue, as well as a group healing experience to ease anxiety.

The common concern about someone not niching themselves is that they won't be memorable. My response: who cares if an acquaintance doesn't understand nor remember what I do? I don't mind that I'm not memorable to random people.

Yet, those who know me personally or my work, tend to promote whatever current thing I'm offering.

Or maybe they remember a particular course of mine that made a difference for them, and they'll share it with friends who have that issue as well.

Therefore, instead of fearing that you won't be known for something specific, put your energy into making a deeper impact in your content and your service towards clients, fans, and friends.

When you give someone a meaningful experience, they have a lot more energy and room in their mind and heart to remember the thing you did that made a positive impact for them.

And that's what they'll tell other people about.

It's like a musician who has multiple albums, dozens of songs. The song I remember – and share – is the one or few songs that made the most difference for me.

They might even produce music in multiple genres, and as a fan I might not connect to most of what they made, but the few pieces that moved my heart? That's what I'll always remember fondly when I think of that band, and that's what I "know them for".

Same thing with you: you can announce dozens of very different offers in the next few years. But each of your clients, fans, friends will only remember the one, or the few, that was most relevant for them.

The offers that weren't relevant for them? They'll have scrolled on by, and probably won't even remember that you offered it. There's way too many other things they saw that day, some of which had more of an impact on them.

That's also the danger of niching your business as a whole: if it's not relevant to your network, they'll forget about your offers anyway, and you only have that one niche to test with them. If however you stay flexible, you get to test many offers, in whichever niches you want to play in, and see what works well for your network.

So, don't fret if you can't niche yourself or your business as a whole. Stay open, stay creative, and play with the edges as much as you'd like. You won't know which new thing you create could become your biggest hit, unless you try it out.

Watch the companion video and add any comments here:

www.bit.ly/abp2ch4

Concentric Circles: A Wholesome Alternative to Sales Funnels

Here's the business model that I use, and recommend for all clients to consider.

It's an alternative to sales funnels (which often feel unethical to me).

This concentric circles model is meant for those who earn a living as a solopreneur. They share their life's experiences via coaching, mentoring, facilitation, or healing.

Here is the model in a single graphic:

www.bit.ly/creatorbizmodel

Notice that there are boundaries to each of the levels in the diagram. The key to making the model work is to set clear boundaries of access at each level, both for your personal sustainability and so your clients have clarity about what support is available at each level.

You

Your authentic business starts with **you** at the center: your knowledge, your creativity, your presence. These are the core assets from which your services and products are developed.

Your energy signature and your work radiate out into the world to add value, doing your part to move humanity forward.

To be personally sustainable in doing your work and to fulfill your potential, it is important to continually learn and deepen your joyful productivity: the more you practice, the more personally sustainable and successful your business will be.

1-1 Clients

1-1 clients are your inner circle. They get the most access to your time and energy.

Of course, we can never be fully responsible for our clients' results, which are largely dependent on their own actions and life circumstances. However, compared to the other levels in the concentric circle model (group program, online courses, etc.), you do have more responsibility for your clients when serving them 1-1. They also pay you at a higher rate here than at other levels.

You can only allow a few 1-1 clients at a time. If your full-time income depends completely on 1-1 clients, the maximum I've seen authentic business owners do is 22-25 hour-long appointments per week. More sustainable is about 15 per week or less.

The success factors of your 1-1 appointments include how effective you are in sessions with clients, and your system for following-up with them.

Ideally, you can supplement your 1-1 work with services/products from other parts of this business model. This brings us to the next level: working with groups.

Group Program

A group coaching or mentoring program may have anywhere from a few people to a few dozen.

My authentic business mentoring group has 80 members, which is large enough to provide a diversity and dynamism that benefits everyone, and yet small enough that I can still track and support every individual throughout the program.

Take a look at the link above. You're welcome to borrow any aspects of my group program to structure your own.

Each of your group members has less access to you than your 1-1 clients. This means you have less responsibility for the results of each group member. The group format emphasizes self-guided learning, where members take more ownership of their progress within the shared framework. Of course, they also pay less than 1-1 clients.

The success factor of your group program will depend on your ability to bring together people of similar values and energy, and your systems for tracking each member's progress.

Some group programs, such as mine, include access to various online courses that the teacher has created, or will create during the program. These online courses could also be sold to those outside the group program.

Online Courses

Whereas a group program must have a limited number of people, online courses are totally scalable. Whether 10 people or 100 people buy your course, it doesn't really take you more work.

If hundreds of people buy your courses, you'll certainly have more student questions to answer, but it's still much less work to have one additional student, compared to one additional group member or one additional 1-1 client. This is what scalability means.

Compared to having clients or group members, you have less responsibility for each student's results since they have even less access to you, and are paying you less than a group member would.

It's important to set clear boundaries of access to you in your business so that you can remain a healthy solopreneur.

For example, the students in my <u>Authentic Business Courses</u> are limited to asking me targeted questions inside the private course platform. Or, they can come to a <u>George Kao Q&A Call</u> once a month. If their question in the course platform is more than I can concisely answer, I ask them to attend the monthly call. This is how I maintain healthy boundaries, while providing enough of my presence to still help my students and provide the value they paid for. Of course, these boundaries are communicated clearly so expectations are clear.

Books

Books (e-books, printed books, audiobooks) are even more scalable than online courses. The price point allows millions of people to buy your books, and readers don't expect that the author will necessarily answer their questions.

If you've read any of my books (<u>George Kao's Books</u>) you know that I offer a link at the end of each chapter that brings them to a place they can comment publicly. This has been a sustainable way for me to provide some light support to my book readers.

Compared to all the previous levels in the Concentric Circle business model – 1 to 1 clients, group programs, and online courses – you should feel even less responsibility for your readers' results. You can't make anyone read, nor implement, your book's advice… much less implement it in the right way.

Yet, you can serve many more people with affordable books compared to your online courses or other services.

Free Content

Finally, the outermost level, where you can reach the most people, is with free content -- things like articles (blog posts), videos, podcasts, or images.

It doesn't cost you anything to have millions of people view your Youtube video or Instagram post. And, if any of your posts go viral and get lots of views, people don't expect that you'll be able to respond to every comment.

At the level of free content, you have the least responsibility for any one person's transformation, and they also expect the least access to you, since it's free. Yet, you can reach the whole world.

Tips

In this business model, should you start with 1-1 clients or with books? If you are needing to make income quickly, getting clients is what I would recommend. If you're not in a hurry to earn income but are building this in your spare time for the long-term, then I'd recommend starting with free content, moving gradually towards 1-1 clients if you wish. In other words, starting from the outside of the concentric circles and going inward towards the innermost circle.

As you study this business model and implement it according to your energy level and priorities, you'll figure out over time how many people you can allow in at each level, and therefore how much you need to charge for each product or service.

Unlike a sales funnel, you welcome people in this model to freely enter or exit any level without pressure to enroll in any other level.

Although I recommend making invitations/announcements of your offers consistently, I hope you'll do it in a gentle way, allowing people to know about something yet being unattached to whether they sign up; this is truly authentic marketing.

Authentic marketing creates a great deal of trust that makes growing your business easier and easier over the years.

May this simple model help you plan your business going forward!

Watch the companion video and add any comments here:

www.bit.ly/abp2ch5

Authentic Email Marketing – Why I Don't Recommend "Lead Magnets"

A common marketing tactic is when you're forced to give your email address in order to access a freebie, like an e-book, webinar, video series, summit, email course, or "special report".

Marketers call this a "lead magnet". Creating a lead magnet means to attract the lead (a human being) with your magnet (your freebie). What an unfortunate term that dissociates marketing from relationship-building.

The real problem? It doesn't even work that well.

I built a 10,000-person email list by using a lead magnet of a "free" webinar.

I put "free" in quotes, because your attention is valuable – not free – and if I require your email address in exchange for my webinar, then you've effectively paid for the webinar with your email.

Then you had to contend with my ongoing emails that tried to sell you on various products & services until you unsubscribed.

Years later, as I transitioned towards authentic marketing, I deleted 90% of my original email list, and only kept the small minority who had engaged recently with my emails.

The people who unknowingly "subscribed" to my email list — when their actual intention was to register for my "free" webinars — were mostly *not* opening my emails. It seems that they cared more about the freebie than ongoing contact with me, which is understandable.

Lead magnets or "ethical bribes" (as they're also called) are a bait-and-switch.

Mostly, the recipient just wants the freebie in the moment, and is not looking forward to ongoing emails.

The average open rate of all email newsletters is about 22%… and yet those of us using "lead magnets" were getting only 10–17% open rates. Dismal.

Now that I've changed my strategy, my email open rates are about 52%, which is more than double the average. More on this later.

It felt demoralizing to realize that the majority of my "subscribers" did not look forward to my emails, no matter how well-written.

It didn't help my creative energy.

Eventually, I made 2 shifts in my email strategy that benefitted my business:

I separated my email lists into Content versus Offers.

I made the sign-up process more intentional.

I'll explain each…

Email Lists for Content vs. Offers

People can subscribe to George Kao's Best Content to receive emails that focus on my free articles and videos… without additional emails about my product launches.

Each newsletter to the people who subscribed to my Best Content does mention *one* offer, but it's deprioritized to the bottom of each email. The reader gets to first see what they expect and want -- the content itself.

On the other hand, people can also join the George Kao Launch List if they want to be sure not to miss the announcements about my upcoming workshops and openings for my coaching.

I created a webpage to give visitors the two newsletter options:

www.GeorgeKao.com/newsletteroptions

After a year, I realized that some subscribers were confused, so now I only publicly promote my Content newsletter.

…and after they sign-up, they receive a confirmation email that *also* mentions the option of joining my Offers email list, if they wish to consider it.

This separation into 2 email lists has worked well for me. My open rates, as well as my click rates, are now much higher than average… giving some evidence that my subscribers are enjoying the new format. ☺

A key principle of authentic marketing is to build a friendly relationship with one's audience... not to force things on them.

A More Intentional Sign-Up Process

When you visit a marketer's website, it's extremely obvious how to sign-up for their email list. The opt-in box is "above the fold" meaning, you don't have to scroll down to see it.

You might even get a pop-up window.

You have to **intentionally avoid** signing up for their email list, if you're not ready to.

And why would you be ready to sign up so soon, when you're just getting to know them? It feels pushy…

I used these tactics in the past.

As I moved into authentic marketing, I decided that I want my audience to **want** my emails, rather than forcing it on them.

If they want my emails, they'll actively look for where they can sign up, and they will join.

So I took **off** the email opt-in box from my homepage.

If visitors are interested enough in my content, they can easily find a Newsletter link in the top navigation bar, or a link in the footer on my webpage.

No more pop-up windows. No more opt-in boxes.

Once they get into the sign-up process, I ask for their email, name, and how they discovered me, as well as what frequency of emails they prefer. Indeed, these questions result in **fewer opt-ins** than if I didn't ask questions... but of the opt-ins I get, they are much more intentional subscribers.

Interestingly, most of my subscribers choose to receive my emails "once a week" instead of "once a month".

Regarding automatic opt-ins, I do make one exception: When someone buys a course from me, they are automatically subscribed to my once-a-month best content newsletter, as well as my offers newsletter, which usually goes out only 2 times per month). It is going well. As I mentioned earlier, my open and click rates are more than *double* the industry average.

What should you do with that freebie you created?

Perhaps you already put in the work to make a freebie. I recommend several options:

1. Make it into a **low-price product**. You were going to "sell" it by asking for an email address anyway… so it's valuable, isn't it? Wouldn't it be worth paying for? That e-book you wrote… publish it on Amazon Kindle. That video series you recorded… make it a low-price course!

2. Even if you don't expect it to make you rich, you can still add a price to it, and **offer it as a bonus** to other services/products you offer (or as a bonus to your friends' services/products if they serve the same audience!)

3. If you don't want to put a price on it, then why not simply make it **ungated content**? Just post it on your website as a blog post or a standalone web page, and share it far and wide. Ungated content is much more likely to be shared and talked about! This gives it the chance to go viral and really bring a lot of ideal visitors to your website. At the bottom of that freebie page, you can include an invitation to receive ongoing great content from you through your email newsletter! This way, taking action to receive ongoing emails is truly intentional, rather than a (somewhat accidental) byproduct of wanting one free thing...

Be sought-after, rather than tolerated.

That's really the bottom line of this transition away from lead-magnets.

Let's do marketing that is sought-after and enjoyed, rather than mildly-annoying and merely tolerated.

You will build an audience of true fans, and a business you can really love!

(Originally written in 2018, updated in 2023.)

Watch the companion video and add any comments here:

www.bit.ly/abp2ch6

Aim not for fame,
but for service.

There's an unspoken assumption in marketing:

More followers/fans lead to more clients, more fulfillment, more freedom.

This is like saying more money equals more happiness.

These are seductive ideas. They contain a grain of truth, but they also come with an unexpected price.

In this chapter I'll share my "more followers" experience. It's not all that it's chalked up to be…

In my first few years in business, I grew my email list to more than 10,000 subscribers.

It led to having some clients, but far fewer than I expected, given my sizable email list audience. I didn't have a full client roster. It also didn't produce much engagement with my content.

However, it did result in many more emails to respond to, more spam to contend with, and more unpaid requests for my time.

Then in 2014, I completely changed my strategy, shifting towards what I consider to be a more "authentic" business. I removed everyone from my list that hadn't opened my emails in more than six months. That accounted for about 90% of my email list! It felt like I started over. (Even the remaining 10% mostly weren't really a good fit with my authentic business.) In a more heart-centered way, grounding my business in a truer spirit of service, trusting God more, I aimed to bring more heart into everything I do.

That deeper commitment to service evolved into my consistent content creation starting in 2015. This resulted in a much truer engagement with my audience.

By the end of 2016, I noticed that I no longer had to reach out to get clients. They were all coming to me now, emailing or messaging me privately and asking about my services. Most of them had discovered me through my consistent creation of authentic content.

Leaning more into a spirit of service, I began to experience deeper fulfillment in my work with clients.

Fewer followers and subscribers also meant fewer emails and fewer unpaid requests on my time… which gave me more freedom.

Now, I am grateful to say that daily, I feel a great sense of well-being, gratitude, and fulfillment in my work, whether I am writing this chapter, or working with a client, or preparing for my next workshop.

This state of inner peace and joy is what I've truly wanted all my life. It is a sweeter experience than any fame and external glory I ever had.

Currently, I only get about a hundred views on my Youtube videos, and a few dozen likes on my best performing FB posts. These are laughable numbers compared with the influencers in my field.

Yet I have a full client roster, a healthy-sized group coaching program, enough workshop participants every time, and my regular content gets meaningful engagement from loyal readers.

I've learned that I don't want to be famous.

I don't really try to get more email subscribers, or fans on Facebook, Youtube, Twitter, etc.

What I do try to do:

- Learn to serve more deeply

- Learn to bring more Love into business

- Learn what you (my audience) find helpful, so I can **be** more helpful

My hope is to be a different kind of role model than the typical business or marketing coach / expert / mentor / speaker / thought-leader / guru you might encounter. They often seem to assume that more fame, more views, more likes, more subscribers, is always better.

You aren't "serving" enough unless you're famous, right?

Notice that seductive thought, then consciously shift towards a deeper way of being in business and marketing, one that fills your heart and soul, rather than boosting ego.

Not more Fame.

More Love.

Greater Truth.

Deeper Service.

May we all aim for – and align our actions towards – our higher callings.

Watch the companion video and add any comments here:

www.bit.ly/abp2ch7

Your business numbers are perfect right now.

Years ago, I launched a program I was very passionate about.

I imagined 20, or 30, maybe even 50 people enrolling and participating. Exciting!

Actual number of sign-ups? One person.

I had to cancel it, and refund the person. It was a painful experience, because my expectations didn't match the results.

A difficult but essential life lesson: to let go of attachment to our plans when reality presents differently.

Looking back, I'm actually glad that the program didn't run. The framework and tools that I teach today are far more efficacious than what I was offering back then. (Good thing I didn't expose more people to the earlier version!)

Today, the program which failed years ago, is now full, with a waiting list. I needed those years to hone my craft, to develop my voice, to practice higher values, and arrive at a deeper perspective about business and marketing.

Oftentimes, we need hindsight to see that we get what we need, not necessarily what we want.

It is a difficult lesson to let go of attachment to our ego's plans.

We think that we *should* have success already: a full client load, a large following of faithful readers, and interest from many people in regards to our work.

I wish for you the greatest of success, truly.

More importantly, I wish for you the peace of having gratitude for whatever stage you are at right now.

How many people read and engage with your posts?

It's the perfect number right now.

How many clients do you have?

It's exactly what you need.

How much money are you making?

It's enough for now.

Of course, things can change quickly. Whenever it changes, the timing is perfect. Even if it takes longer than planned, it is still just right.

We truly don't know what it is we need for our growth, even if we think we know. To remember that is to practice humility.

Whatever stage we're at is where we need to be, because if we had truly learned the lessons of this current stage, we would have advanced to a further stage. As you adequately integrate your experience and improve your skills, you'll move forward.

Imagine that you're a white belt in martial arts, dreaming of being a black belt. It's a good thing that right now you aren't thrown into black belt situations! You'd get really hurt with your skills as is. Thankfully, you're still in the white belt class.

When I'm in a healthy state of mind, I think of myself as being one of the beginning belts, knowing that there is much more to learn. I'm grateful for whatever class I'm qualified to be in right now.

We are called to humbly walk the journey of authentic business:

- To create content to keep exploring our voice and honing our ideas

- To keep connecting with those we think we can help

- To consistently (and lightly!) launch our offerings

- To remember that offerings are always an exploration of that magical intersection between our passion and the market's wants

- To continually seek feedback on what we do

…so that we can continually improve our content and offerings

All along the way, to keep appreciating where we are, knowing it's where we need to be.

Daily being in appreciation, then stretching. This is how we keep moving forward with a positive mindset and uplifting emotions. Putting it into 2 tangible steps to do daily in order to integrate this energetic:

1. Practice gratitude and love for where you are now.

2. Stretch towards your infinite potential.

With every launch, you are getting clearer about your true livelihood.

Step by step, you are living into your calling.

Always remember: you are being lifted and guided by a higher power that can see farther and deeper than you, and knows exactly what you need at this time.

Where you are right now is perfect. Whatever the enrollment numbers. Whatever the size of your following.

Keep creating, listening, launching, adapting, and appreciating.

More importantly, I wish for you the peace of gratitude.

Watch the companion video and add any comments here:

www.bit.ly/abp2ch8

Should you "Charge what you're worth"?

Have you heard that in your pricing, you should *"stand up for your value"* ?

Let's reflect on this:

How much is your value?

How much are you worth?

$25/hour? $250/hour? $500/hour? $10,000/hour?

Words matter. They shape how we see ourselves and others. Connecting our fees to our "worth" is a deeply unhealthy comparison.

Are you worth *less* than someone who charges more?

Truth: You are worth infinity.

You are a precious human being whose odds of being born are 1 in 400 trillion!

I always wonder whether "charge what you're worth" was started by some high-priced coach who needed to justify how much they're charging…

I have seen many people raise their prices because they're "worth" more! And then what happened? Their rates became unsustainable for the vast majority of their audience. They had to lower their prices, and felt very conflicted about it, because they had unwittingly connected their rates to their self-esteem.

So let's stop using the word "worth" in connection to our fees.

Consider this more practical idea:

"Charge based on the market rate."

It makes sense to set your price based on what your clients are expecting and seeing in the marketplace.

Look at your colleagues and what they're charging. Then look at your own needs. Price your services accordingly.

Then, based on the market's response, you might need to change your pricing.

There is such a thing as perceived value. If you have more premium branding and copywriting, people are usually willing to pay more.

However, before we all rush to rebrand ourselves as a premium / luxury service, we need to consider whether that would be authentic to how we wish to show up in the world.

Let's look at another common idea:

"Charge what the market will bear."

Economics teaches us to charge the maximum amount that our clients will tolerate…

Let's flip this around and apply **The Golden Rule**—You are my market, my potential clients. How would you feel if I charged you the biggest amount you could bear?

This is what some high-price coaches and programs do. They charge as much as they can get away with…

Their justification: "When the client pays *more*, they'll take it *more* seriously and get *more* results." Really? Are they using this line of thinking to justify their own self-enrichment? The truth is that most people who pay for high-priced programs *don't* get the results promised.

Guess what? I used to do all this. I used to teach it, too. I've also worked with many colleagues who operated from this mindset.

This is how business is *supposed* to work, right? Everyone is supposed to be *out for themselves.* The sellers should charge more, and buyers should beware...

I don't like this adversarial relationship between a business and its customer. I stand for a more caring vision: what if business owners could have compassion for their customers and customers could also care about taking care of the business owner, too? Wouldn't that be a better world, one where everyone is elevated?

We can achieve this vision. We just need to remember that it's not how most businesses are run, and we need to take a stand if we want to create something different.

Here are some other common lies about what to charge in your business:

"Charge *not* for your time, but for the *value* you provide."

So, if you're a marriage coach who helps people avoid divorce, how much is that worth? Or an occupational therapist who helps someone recover their ability to work. How much value is in that outcome?

These results could be worth **hundreds of thousands** of dollars. It's ridiculous to price your services "based on the value you provide"... and your potential clients will think so too.

Higher Prices = Higher Quality?

"People have the idea that if something costs more, it must be *better* than a cheaper version." It's possible people will think that, until they try the product or service and are disappointed... and then word of mouth spreads.

When you charge more, people *expect* more, and are more quickly disappointed. When expectations are high, you run a higher risk of underdelivering.

When you charge less however, people expect less, and are **delighted** when they receive great service from you. This brings positive word-of-mouth. They'll talk to their friends about what a great deal your service is!

Take a deep breath…

…and remember that we are all in this together. There are a lot of lies and misconceptions about what to charge.

As an authentic business owner, let us aim to operate our businesses to support the birthing of a more compassionate world.

A few years ago, I underwent a personal transformation, and it resulted in a profound shift of intent and motivation. My business priorities changed from "more profit" towards authenticity, service, and fulfillment.

I no longer want to charge "what I'm worth" or "what the market will bear."

Instead:

I charge based on Enoughness and Compassion.

Do I have what I need?

And, can I work on lessening my financial needs, finding fulfillment in my (inner) life, and in serving my community?

My financial reality is that for 20 years I've lived in San Francisco. It's been expensive compared to most places. Yet as of this writing, I've just moved to Mexico! It's been only a short time, but I can already see that my lifestyle here will cost less. This means that I will be able to pass on the savings onto my clients, and/or offer more profit sharing to my affiliates, many of whom are my clients!

Even so, while living in San Francisco, I was still able to charge less than most peers at my level. I made sure my lifestyle allowed it.

Should you charge *less* than your peers? It depends on your needs, and your reputation.

Your audience might feel that you are so unique that you cannot be compared. This is why I always advocate for getting better at your authentic content marketing. Can you authentically, with integrity, position your service next to higher-priced peers? If so, then you should, because it's true.

Compassion in Pricing

Besides Enoughness, I try to integrate Compassion into my pricing. We've all had the following two experiences…

Experience 1. We want to buy a service, but we see the price and we think "Wow! That's expensive." As we think about making the payments, we might feel stressed.

Experience 2. We love a service, and we feel the pricing is so affordable. *"This is such a good deal! I would happily tell others about this service!"* We feel relieved by their pricing… grateful… and we become *advocates* of their business. This is **reciprocal compassion** at work: the seller charges compassionately, and the buyer feels they want to take care of the business' well-being, by adding a gratuity (an expression of gratitude) or by spreading the word.

Two comments I received from readers of an earlier version of this chapter:

"George, when I first saw your pricing for your courses, I wondered "Is he missing a 0 in there?!" I definitely was full of relief as I had already spent too much on other programs that were way overpriced!!"

"…same! It's such a relief to purchase something affordable that's so high quality. It makes me really appreciate my investment and as a result, I've just bought more!"

I hope we can all give our audience that experience — "What a great deal!"

Important also is to remember, as we discussed in the Concentric Circle business model in an earlier chapter, that our 1–1 service does not need to be the lowest-price thing we offer. In fact, because it gives customers the most access to you, and you have the most responsibility for their results, a great deal for 1-1 service can be higher. Youcan also offer books, workshops, or group programs at lower prices, which may then give your audience that feeling of relief and gratitude, while still giving them the benefit of our work. To recap the Concentric Circle business model, which is my recommended business model for solopreneurs, go back to that chapter.

The bottom line—separate your fees from your "worth". Aim to charge from enoughness and compassion. Build a clientele and audience that feels deep gratitude for your offerings.

(Originally written in 2018, updated in 2023.)

Watch the companion video and add any comments here:

www.bit.ly/abp2ch9

ART (Alignment, Reach, Trust) - Levers to Grow Your Authentic Business

Imagine three levers that can help grow your authentic business: Alignment, Reach, and Trust.

Increasing any one of them can help, but the best results come from increasing all three evenly.

Alignment

This means that you have offers and content that are aligned with what your audience wants. How do you know? The more aligned, the more your audience is engaged with your offers and content.

Where solopreneurs often get disappointing results is when they launch offers based on their own inspiration and interests, yet they haven't done enough market research to create a product/service that is well-aligned with what their audience wants. This is why they get so little response from people.

To increase alignment, work on:

1. Market research conversations with your audience. (My courses that cover this: CORE and Offer Revision.)

2. Polling your audience so you can co-create various aspects of your offer, such as the title of a course or product.

3. Netcaring with your nichemates to discover what's working for them in terms of their offers. They can also learn from you as well, and you can grow together.

Reach

This second lever is your ability to reach, at will, enough of the right people who are aligned with your offers and content, to therefore have enough engagement and sales.

This is a common pitfall for solopreneurs – not having enough people who are seeing their good content and offers. Reach is what we are working on when we learn to distribute content and do collaborations with other content creators.

Here are my 7 favorite reach strategies. Because these are methods that have worked well for me I do teach a course on each of these:

1. FB Ads

2. IG Ads

3. Stage 2 Content

4. Gentle Launches

5. Collabs

6. LinkedIn Ads

7. Authentic SEO

Each of these methods has great potential. Each method could get you all the clients you ever need, if you use it well.

The following are not what I mean by "reach" strategies:

- YouTube – unless you're going to get great at YT SEO (quite difficult) and be willing to study their retention graphs and do a lot of video editing…

- Your own email list is not what I consider "reach" – and neither is simply posting on social media – in both cases, they're *already* part of your audience... you're not really growing your reach unless you use one of the 7 methods above.

Trust

How much trust does your audience have in your abilities, presence, and values?

The deeper their trust, the less Alignment or Reach you need to work hard at. Or another way to put it: the more trust you have with people, the more likely they'll help you with alignment and reach.

Many solopreneurs get persuaded or charmed to work with mainstream marketers who teach them methods that actually erode trust with their people, and thereby, they can't build sustainable and trusting audiences.

The trust has not been earned, so business remains difficult over the years.

To nurture trust, work on:

1. <u>Joyful Productivity</u> practices

2. <u>Healthy Money</u> practices

3. <u>Consistently creating content</u>, especially authentic videos

4. <u>Netcaring with nichemates</u> from a place of genuine enjoyment

5. <u>Mastery of your craft</u>

Trust > Reach > Alignment

In practice, though, I like to recommend working on T then R then A.

Trust comes through consistently showing up with authentic content and skillful client work. Consistency of action will grow your own trust in yourself, which then spills over into others' trust in you.

Reach methods – different ways to distribute content and offers – becomes more effective (better time & money spent) the more you have trustworthy content and offers.

Alignment becomes easier as you grow your reach. The bigger your audience, the more accurate your polls about your offers & content, and the more likely you'll get Yes's when reading out for market research conversations. The research allows you to create even better Offers and Content, which then grows your Trust. This creates a virtuous cycle, where the trust of the audience leads to better alignment and reach… which in turn leads to greater trust.

I hope that this basic framework will give you some helpful direction to grow your authentic business!

Watch the companion video and add any comments here:

www.bit.ly/abp2ch13

Authentic Creativity & Making Money

"I long for the ability to create without any thoughts of money…to create because I love it… to take real time off when I need it… to try new things and build in more hobby-time into my life.

Although everything I create is because I love it, I tend to always have that background question: 'Will it make me money?'

I want to get to a place where I feel I can try things and fail and be totally fine with it…"

–a reader sent this to me.

Indeed, it's a life that many of us heart-based people long for. It's a worthy vision, and it's absolutely possible – step by step. We can even do some of it now, without having to wait.

Let's first distinguish two activities:

Hobbies can be a creative and personal endeavor, with no pressure for anyone to buy, or even like, our work.

Business, however, has the need to sustain itself which requires enough people to buy into our work. There's some pressure for meeting others' wants.

As you continue building your audience, the pressure in business should decrease. There will come a time when you'll finally have plenty of true fans -- those who are willing to buy just about anything you sell.

Through my content and courses, this is what I aim to help you do—create your own true fan audience—because that's when you will have true **creative freedom** in your business.

Yet, building that kind of audience takes more time than you've probably been sold. It requires strategic actions, taken consistently, including content creation, audience research, collaborations…

It's a journey, so let's not expect overnight success. Maybe you have 2 or 3 clients who already buy much of what you create and sell. Maybe next year you'll have 10 or 12 such clients. (With diligence and a bit of luck, you might be able to speed up the process and get to perhaps 20 next year, maybe even more.)

While we are on the journey toward financial sustainability, how can we relate to money-making without desperation?

For us to be creative, and to serve deeply, money needs to be an *afterthought*.

You need to get a secure income before you can really explore and serve freely, i.e. to build an authentic business.

Basic financial security allows you to ***then*** focus on truly serving your customers, which then further expands your financial resources.

It's like the sailboat metaphor by Scott Kaufman—if you haven't secured the leaks in your boat (that are endangering your life) then it's all you can think about.

Financial stability happens with one of these:

(1) Require less income – live more simply – which will engage and require your creativity and discipline.

(2) Make more income from one of these sources: getting a job, getting a promotion, or selling easier products in your business.

In the entrepreneurial world there's been too much judgment about working in a job. No shame in it. Use the job to build a bridge toward entrepreneurship, by working bit by bit on your business in your spare time.

Or if you're already full-time dedicated to your business, there's no shame in selling what you know is *easier to sell* to make money. Create the stability that allows you to then experiment with things that ***might not*** make money.

A side note on selling what's easier – it may be that you simply need to lower your hourly rate so that people have no qualms about signing up to try your service, then they'll see how great you are and spread the word. For example, if you're having a hard time getting enough clients at $100/hour, what if you temporarily lowered your rate to $50 or even $30 per hour? You'll probably fill your client roster. Then, gradually increase your price again. See: the tapering strategy for getting clients.

Desperation happens when you require your security to come from a project you've never succeeded at before.

For any business project that is new or creative, be in *the energy of curiosity and alignment.*

1. Curiosity: "I wonder if this will serve their wants enough for them to buy it?"… the intention is to experiment with creatively meeting them where they're at.

2. Alignment: "How can I structure the pricing and marketing so that there will be enough visibility and exchange to make it a win for both them and me?"

This means you need to look at new business projects as *experiments*, not as certainties for income. It's a chance to practice curiosity and alignment, but as is true with all practice: many so-called "mistakes" or "failures" are necessary before you get it right. If you can frame it all as learning experiences, you will benefit and grow.

Another apt analogy is **breathing**: if you're barely breathing, you have no energy to be creative nor to give to others. Be gentle with yourself. Having a stable income is like having enough breath. Work on that first—

get an easy job or sell what's easy—before you try to be super creative in your business.

If you can't stand your job, you need to either:

1. see that job as a blessing for now—giving you income stability, plus a daily opportunity to practice joyful productivity…

2. or spend enough time on the evenings/weekends to find another stable job that is more acceptable to you.

Whatever you choose, remember this:

Every single day, wherever you work, there is the opportunity for you to **practice inner development** (mindfulness, embodied virtues, etc) and at the same time, to **make a positive difference** in the lives of those you work with. No matter what work you do, the freedom to *practice and grow* is always available.

Watch the companion video and add any comments here:

www.bit.ly/abp2ch16

Niche mates, not competitors.

How do you feel about the word "competition"? For us self-employed people, that word can create anxiety and resistance. Being "competitive" tends to make human beings less cooperative.

Instead, I recommend using the term "niche mates" — other worthy human beings who occupy the same industry niche as us.

They, too, have families to feed, and dreams they hope to achieve. And, similar to us, they also have hidden suffering in their life that, if we only knew, would inspire our deep compassion.

The world is starving for genuine, win-win collaborations.

Let's find a better way to think about, and work with, our niche mates.

There are essentially 3 options:

1. Niche mates can fight each other. Or at least, fear each other, generating discouragement and avoidance. Sometimes, even aggression, when people talk badly about their competitors.

2. Or, we can observe each other's business behavior, and learn from that, since we are serving similar people using similar skills.

3. Even better is that if we get creative, we can figure out a way to grow our niche together by collaborating.

Because the word "competitor" is the default way people think about others in their niche, they default to the first option of avoidance or aggression.

If a little wiser, they might get "strategic" and try the second option: learning from their competition, but even so, it's often out of hoping that the competition will eventually lose.

Let's be more mindful in how we think about our niche mates, and focus instead on learning and collaborating.

We can all have enough

Every single business can have enough clients, if we become more mindful, active, and caring about creating win-win relationships.

A niche mate is another business, like you, that provides a service similar to what you provide, and which serves a similar audience.

A niche mate, like you, has both insecurities and genius zones (that might complement yours.) They need to support themselves, as you do, and might have a family to support. Your niche mates deserve good opportunities. And, like you, your niche mates also need and deserve help.

In fact, your niche mates are either your best mirrors, or your best partners.

Niche Mates as Mirrors

It's difficult to see how good (or bad) you look, and adjust your appearance, unless you look into a mirror.

Similarly, it's hard to figure out the best ways to improve your own branding, messaging, and marketing, unless you look at your niche mates. They are essentially mirrors for your business!

When you look at your niche mates, you're naturally able to critique and praise.

Do you love something they're doing? Then do more of it yourself. (Not copying, but emulating, in your own style and with your own voice.)

Do you dislike something they're doing? Take that silent criticism and refrain from doing it in your own business, too. (If you are friendly with them, and they seem open to your feedback, you might help them by offering constructive critique.)

Study Your Niche Mates

Ask around your network for who else does similar work that you do.

Write down the names of 5 niche mates…

For each, answer these questions:

- What are 2 things you like about their services, which you might want to emulate?

- What's broken? What's missing? What's unnecessary?

- What's unique about your services that sets you apart from them?

- What are 2 things you like about their marketing?

- What are 2 things you don't like about their marketing?

- What's unique about your marketing that sets you apart from them?

- Are you addressing the same audience? Or what's different about yours?

- What could they be doing differently or better to meet their audience's needs?

From these insights, you can then modify and improve your own business.

Instead of copying, focus on being of service…

Don't try to match your niche mates' offerings, feature by feature.

For each feature they provide in their service, ask yourself how it is trying to solve a problem for the clients you both serve.

Contemplate these questions:

- Is there a better way to solve this problem?

- Can I solve it in a different way, in my own style, with my own experience and wisdom?

- Can I solve it in a way that is more effective or delightful, based on what I know about my clients?

Focus on solving your ideal clients' needs in the best way you know how.

Niche Mates as Partners

When you find a niche mate that has a similar-sized audience as you, contact them casually, and ask if they would be open to finding ways to collaborate or mutually support each other.

Some people might not respond. That's ok. The few who do respond positively, are abundance-minded like you. Good opportunity to make a new friend!

Why our niche mates can be some of our best partners:

- Do your offerings complement each other? Perhaps your offers can help each other's

audience in different ways or styles that are both
important.

- Your audience has some people who don't (and
  will never) buy from you — it's just statistics —
  and this is true for your niche mates, too. Yet,
  those same non-buyers may love to buy from
  your niche mate if they are endorsed by you…
  and vice versa. In other words, you can refer
  business to each other!

Again, focus on contacting niche mates with a similar-
sized audience as you, whatever you can tell of their
numbers based on looking at their social media profiles.

If they're open to collaborating, then help each by
introducing content or offerings to each other's audience,
so that everyone can be helped:

1. That audience is helped by having an alternative
    that may work better for them.

2. Someone is helped by gaining a new client (or at
    least, a new reader/viewer.)

3. The introducer benefits by building trust with all
    parties involved.

A client who buys something is likely to buy another
similar thing. The person who follows a topic will enjoy
discovering another creator in the same field. Partnering
with niche mates can be a win for everyone.

In your research into niche mates, also take note of who is partnering with your niche mates? Who is endorsing them, or introducing your niche mates' offerings to their audience? They might also be interested in introducing your offerings, too.

If we connect & share, there is more than enough for everyone. There are always more than enough ideal clients. We just need to be more active and caring in connecting with our niche mates.

Watch the companion video and add any comments here:

www.bit.ly/abp2ch17

"Do what you love" …vs… "Offer what they want" – Passion vs. *Compassion* in an Authentic Business

This is a common idea among solopreneurs:

"If I have a passion for something, then there **must** be enough other people with that passion, which means I can build a viable business."

Building a business on *passion* alone can take much longer than you initially think it would. You might have to search far and wide for individuals with a passion like yours. Then, you have to build enough trust for them to buy from you.

Or instead of finding people already passionate in what you have passion for, you can build an online audience from scratch – people who resonate with your energy signature – and then educate them until they really "get" why you're so passionate about your topic.

These are viable paths, but they take more time than most people want.

To create income sooner, consider a *compassion-focused* (or market-led) business.

Yes, there are two different focuses when building an Authentic Business:

Passion Focus—creating a product/service from what energizes **you**, from the philosophies, ideas, strategies that you love... your own background, knowledge, trainings you've received, peak experiences you've had, topics you enjoy talking about. In short, your passions. *"Do what you love."* This requires a long-term effort to grow and nurture a large warm audience.

Compassion Focus—creating a product/service based on what energizes your existing audience/network. *Actual* problems, challenges, issues, frustrations, and yearnings that are facing the people you already know, and can therefore reach easily. *"Offer what they want."* This creates a financially-viable business sooner.

Passion says:

"I think the world needs this."

"I believe people need that."

Compassion says:

"What are people saying they want?"

"What problems are they trying to solve?"

If people aren't eagerly buying what you're selling, you might be leaning too much on your passion. In other words, ask yourself whether you're stuck in your own head.

On the other hand, a *compassion* focus comes from **real individuals you have talked with.** You know their names, you know enough about their life to know the actual problems they face, and you've talked with them enough to know how they describe those problems.

You know enough to design (or re-design) an offer that resonates with them.

Two Sources of Energy

Another way to put it is that there are 2 sources of energy that move your business:

1. **Internal** – your own experiences, skills, intuitions, and passion.

2. **External** – the struggles, yearnings, and buying patterns of the people you're in touch with.

Those who lean too much on external energy, even though they might see more impact and income, are in danger of abandoning the soul of their business.

On the other hand, many heart-based people lean very much on their internal energy to try to build their business, and the danger is burnout because there's often not enough energy to make the business viable. An important part of business energy is money, which comes from other people spending on your product or service.

Compassion (Com-Passion) = "To Suffer With"

Consider the last time you felt moved to help someone who was suffering.

Or think of a time when you got excited about someone's dream/vision, and you felt inspired to help their journey.

You were energized by *compassion*. You were motivated by what someone else was wanting.

And that's a wise thing to do in business too, because *your income is derived from other people's spending.*

People spend on what *they* want, not necessarily what *you* are passionate about.

So when you build a business from a **compassion focus**, you tend to get clients sooner. Your marketing becomes about giving people what they want.

"Being a nice person" vs. Focused Empathy

"I'm such a nice person, I do **so much** for other people, but I'm still not making any money."

This is an issue of focused compassion versus diffused. Maybe you spend time helping just about anyone who asks you, rather than practicing stronger boundaries, and focusing on helping just your ideal client type. (Outside of business hours you can do anything you want, but what makes business viable is spending time on helping the ideal type of client.)

Or maybe you haven't turned your focused compassion into a product/service, so you're just giving and giving without monetizing. That sounds like a hobby, or volunteering. If you want a viable business, you need to charge for some of your compassionate labor.

For better and worse, money is society's allocation signal for what it considers "valuable" work. People are spending money where they *want* the work to be done. Therefore, notice where your ideal clients are spending the money, and design your offers accordingly.

Again, if you *don't* need income, then you can develop your "business" (really, a hobby that could become a business over time and with enough investment of your energy and money) from your own passions and ideas. That *can* lead to income, but it will typically require a much longer-term investment before you see financial returns.

Eventually you may find a sweet spot: the combination of the two.

Passion + compassion creates a genuinely **authentic business.** It is being able to do what you love, and talk about it in a way that others understand and love to buy.

However, it usually starts with either passion (a long road to financial viability) or focused compassion (listening to the market.)

You can *flavor* your market-led work with your passion.

Even if you must make income now, and are "forced" to create a market-focused business, you can still bring elements of your Passion in order to flavor your paid work, to make it more meaningful, unique, enjoyable.

Example:

Even as I coach people on business/marketing, I enjoy talking & writing about spirituality and personal growth.

Even though my clients won't pay me to talk about those personal topics ;-) they do enjoy it when I bring in spiritual values. It makes me a unique business coach for them.

Still, they are paying me for the *business* expertise… not for my philosophizing!

I share my opinions and values to make work more *meaningful* for me, and more *unique* to them.

Another example:

A musician may have passion for a particular new song he wrote.

And yet, his audience wants to hear him play the old favorites.

If he wants to keep his audience coming back, he will play the old faves, hence the Compassion for the audience. He can flavor those performances with his own style.

And of course, once he has his audience's interest, he can also introduce his passion for his own songs.

Finding Your Purpose through Compassion

A reader of this chapter wrote:

"Another point is that when you choose your audience first -- one that you care about -- your passion may find you. As you strive to help them succeed or overcome their obstacles you find purpose and fulfillment in the work you do.

I'm reminded of the story of the hospital janitor who was observed diligently -- and happily -- attending to a coma patient's room: cleaning, restocking medical supplies, and even placing flowers by the bed. When asked how he could be so happy about this apparently mundane job he enthusiastically replied, 'I'm helping the patient get better! Studies show that patients who wake up in a warm environment get better more quickly. Those who don't often go downhill fast. I'm making sure that the doctor has everything he needs to provide the best care and that the patient is in the best environment to recover.'

The janitor linked his work to the patient's recovery, not his paycheck. He reframed his work into a purpose larger than himself and in doing so, found passion."

–Paul Sampang

Always Aim to Integrate

If your passion isn't paying the bills yet, make it a hobby for now.

Make your paid work (focused compassion) more *interesting* by bringing aspects of your hobby (passion) to it, like how I bring spirituality into business coaching.

Experiment and play with it; bring your creativity to it!

The aim of Authentic Business is to gradually bring the two into perfect alignment: your passion + compassion.

Originally published June 6, 2018. Updated in 2023.

Watch the companion video and add any comments here:

www.bit.ly/abp2ch18

The Tao of Authentic Business

I was getting ready to launch my podcast and I sought a good name for it. My audience suggested the playful name of "Business Tao with George Kao".

Some were concerned that the podcast name might be cultural/religious appropriation. (Nevermind that I'm Chinese, and can pronounce Tao te Ching more accurately than most Western Taoist scholars, and that Taoism is characteristically unattached from definitions and who gets credit for what…)

Still, the question inspired me to dive back into studying Taoist philosophical principles. In this chapter, I'll briefly share how a few such principles might apply to Authentic Business.

Authenticity

A core principle of Taoism is to live authentically. To sense into how the flow of Life is calling to us, and to merge with that flow.

As applied to business, this is well-aligned with my teachings of Authentic Business: to create and sell that which is deeply meaningful -- life giving -- for us, and to do marketing "authentically" which is to give into the natural yearning to connect to other people in play and service.

This is as opposed to *in*authentic business -- mainstream business which measures success by profit rather than by authentic meaning.

Also, conventional marketing is about forcing (by way of persuasion) others to do what is profitable for our business, rather than by merging with others in the flow of play and service, which is what authentic marketing is all about.

Detachment

To *not* resist results, aka reality, the natural flow of life.

In conventional business, objectives and goals must be met to be considered "successful".

For authentic businesses, we aim to find value in the action itself. Whether we are writing, selling, serving clients, or doing admin work, we aim to bring joyful productivity to it. We work on our compassionate service, our playful exploration, and by doing so, the process of building a business *itself* becomes worthwhile, regardless of today's results or tomorrow's projections.

We consider every day a success because we get to learn more about ourselves and about the world, and to practice embodying our values in our actions.

We know that good results will eventually manifest when we act in alignment with authentic business. There's no egoic attachment to a specific profit timeline.

Sure, we can make projections, but those are done in a playful way, with curiosity about how they will match with actual metrics.

Business metrics are measurements of reality. Observing them teaches us about the flow of the market. Goals are aspirations toward how we can develop ourselves -- what kind of people we can become -- because results come naturally from a developed business.

(Another application of detachment: I don't copyright any of my writings.)

Effortlessness

One of the popular principles of Taoism is "wu wei" which has been defined in various ways -- natural action, non-action, inexertion, inaction, or effortless action.

To me, this is the combination of authenticity and detachment. When I write this chapter, for example, I am not attached to whether or not my audience likes it. I am writing because I have an authentic interest to do it. I am not contorting myself into performing for others. I am working, yes, and I'm taking action, yes, but I'm doing it more from an attitude of curious exploration -- the play of a child!

When I'm doing bookkeeping, I'm curious about the numbers and how they'll turn out. When I'm clearing my emails, I play with the balance of compassion and boundaries, rather than "work hard" at clearing my emails. When I'm meeting with clients or teaching a course, I am either feeling into what needs to be said in the moment, or following a course outline. Either way, there's no mental anguish for how I "must" manifest results.

In all my business actions, the "work" I do is to bring my heart and Spirit into the moment… and then let that guide my hands and my mouth.

Self-Discipline

A discussion of Taoism wouldn't be complete without the concept of self-discipline. Taoist masters practice self-healing and various rituals in a disciplined manner.

Yet how is self-discipline "going with the flow"?

Look at nature: it is extraordinarily disciplined. Without fail, the sun rises everyday. Water follows gravity, always. Animals have consistent rhythms of resting, hunting, migrating.

Only human beings have minds that give us so much freedom that we can choose to have our own rhythms -- or to ignore them.

Lao Tzu says:

"Don't think you can attain total awareness and whole enlightenment without proper discipline and practice. This is egomania. Appropriate rituals channel your emotions and life energy toward the light. Without the discipline to practice them, you will tumble constantly backward into darkness."

One of the key aspects of authentic business is joyful productivity. I work even when I don't feel like it, yet my work in that moment is to bring virtue and play into the task. In other words, I'm strict about showing up, but lenient about the results.

I also *rest* before I need to, take breaks and naps even when I don't feel like it, because I know that only with proper rhythms of rest can health (and business) thrive.

***

Even so, I know that I am only cherry-picking a few ideas from Taoism, and not doing it justice.

Still, there must be a good reason that my audience suggested Business Tao with George Kao and then voted for it 37-to-4.

I hope this chapter contributes a little to bringing those principles into business.

Watch companion video and add any comments here:

www.bit.ly/abp2ch19

How much should you spend on coaching / mentoring for your business and marketing?

Someone asked what I thought about paying $20,000 per year for a business coach…

Of course, it's fine if you're having a very worthwhile experience, and if you are gradually paying for it. My concern is when you're **paying a large sum** and the coach is new to you, yet promising you the sun, the moon, and the stars.

Many of us idealistic business owners are easily taken by big promises from authoritative-looking coaches. We can end up wasting thousands… or tens of thousands of dollars.

The money you spend for business coaching should really be going towards these five areas:

1. **Knowledge** from someone whose experience and wisdom you respect.

2. **Accountability** to them (or someone else) for you to apply that knowledge.

3. **Customization** and **troubleshooting** to work through the inevitable challenges and unexpected situations as you try to apply the knowledge.

4. **Software** to automate some business processes, to save you time. However, to have an authentic business, you should refrain from automating some tasks such as the actual creation of your content and offers, and personal interaction with your audience.

5. **Outsourcing** to freelancers the processes that you can't automate or that are too technical for you.

A good business coach might be able to deliver all of the above for you… but there are smarter ways to do this.

Rather than paying someone a lot of money up front, I recommend smaller amounts first. Test out their cheapest services/products, and then gradually pay more as they *earn your trust* and you experience for yourself how worthwhile their offerings are.

If you had a $20,000 budget for coaching, it would be better to segment that 20K and give 1K to 20 different coaches to experience a variety of personalities and modalities and see what fits you best.

Or give $500 to 10 different coaches ($5K total) before you invest more in the best three of those candidates. That way, you get a diversity of insight and methods, and you'll be more likely to find something that works well for you.

Without experiencing a variety of ways that people coach you, how do you know what kind of business coaching fits you best?

As for the 5 deliverables I described above, there are more efficient ways that don't require paying large sums to a coach:

1. **Knowledge** can be received through online courses, which are several hundred dollars, instead of thousands. I teach many courses for authentic solopreneurs.

2. **Accountability** can be done through focusmate. It's very affordable.

3. **Customization** and **troubleshooting** can be accomplished through a coaching group that has many experienced peers to offer feedback. Instead of paying $20K, I charge about one-tenth of that for my coaching group: George Kao Group Coaching.

4. **Software** should be part of your budget, since it can save you so much time. Simplero is my top choice for an all-in-one platform to handle website, mailing list, course delivery, client management, and affiliate tracking.

5. **Outsourcing** can be done cheaply and effectively through Fiverr.

All of that combined can add up to less than $10,000 a year, saving you another $10K that you can put towards other types of services… or simply take a much needed vacation!

Watch companion video and add any comments here:

www.bit.ly/abp2ch20

Acknowledgements

Two friends read the manuscript and gave me thoughtful feedback:

Ali Katz – https://linktr.ee/alikatz

Andrea J. Lee – https://andreajlee.com

Both of these amazing individuals are highly experienced authentic business builders. I am deeply honored for their support of this book. Go and check out their wonderful work!

To all of my clients: I honor your dedication to your true livelihood! I witness your willingness to continually grow into greater effectiveness as an authentic business owner and human being.

To my course participants: Thank you for your sincere engagement with the material and your thoughtful questions. You are helping me become a better teacher.

To those who watch my videos and read my posts: Each time I see your views, likes and comments, it encourages me and inspires me to create better content. Your questions and comments have helped to make the content of this book!

To my referral partners: I'm deeply grateful for your trust in my ability to help those you send to me. I'll continue to do my best to make you proud.

Last and certainly not least – to my wife: my heartfelt
gratitude for your loyal support and love!

About The Author

Since 2009, George Kao has been a marketing mentor, consultant, and coach to small business owners, speakers, and authors.

George's mission is to raise the marketing effectiveness (and authentic selling!) of those who prioritize integrity, compassion, and generosity in their business.

George teaches online courses about authentic online marketing, including advertising, authentic content creation, defining your offerings, how to create and market courses, and joyful productivity. You can find all his current courses at www.GeorgeKao.com/Courses

To receive a regular email newsletter with George's best articles, visit www.GeorgeKao.com/Newsletter

www.ingramcontent.com/pod-product-compliance
Lightning Source LLC
Chambersburg PA
CBHW060105260726

48658CB00004B/1415